Playing Football

Written by Philippa Jean
Illustrated by Kate Ellis

Joshua loves playing football.
On Tuesdays he goes
to football practice
and on Saturdays he plays
with his team, the Tigers.

Joshua has a friend called
Alex.
Alex's dad gives him
a pound every time he scores
a goal.

Alex scores lots of goals
and he gets lots of pounds.

Last Saturday,
Joshua scored a goal.
He asked his dad for a pound.

His dad said,
"Yes, you can have a pound,
Joshua, if you share it
with the other kids on the team.
They all helped you.
They passed the ball to you.
They helped you to get the goa

"But Dad..." said Joshua.

"That's fair, isn't it?" asked Dad.

"Yes, it is," said Joshua.
"I'm going to have a talk with Alex!"